There are five kinds of conchs that live in the warm waters of the Caribbean Sea.
The *Fighting Conch* has a strong shell with a thick lip.
The *Milk Conch* has a lip that is often as white as milk.
The *Hawkwing Conch* has fine ribs on the back of its lip that make it look like a bird's wing.
The *Roostertail Conch* is so named because its lip is curved high like the tail of a rooster.
But the *Queen Conch* is the most beautiful of all. Its pink lip shines with shades of peach, rose and gold.
This book is about a Queen Conch.

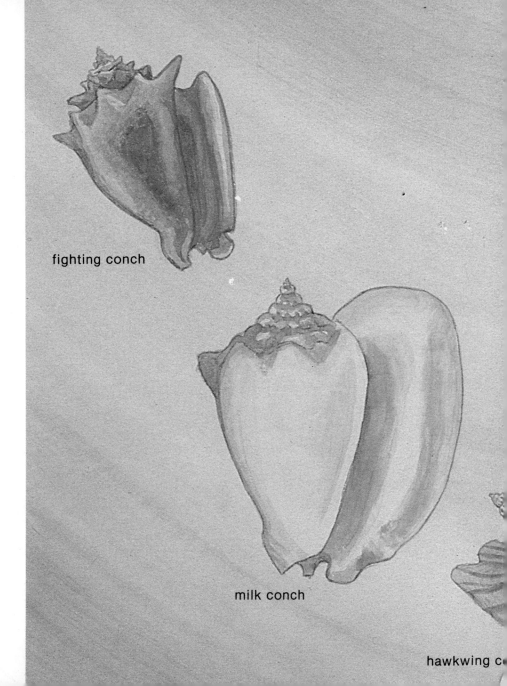

fighting conch

milk conch

hawkwing c

SHELLEY

Katherine Orr

MACMILLAN CARIBBEAN

roostertail conch

queen conch

Queen Conchs are very special.
Their shells are sold in stores all over the world and people wear jewellery made from conch shells.
Their meat is sweet and white.
The people of the Caribbean have always fished for conchs to help feed their families.
More and more people are fishing for conchs and conchs are now harder and harder to find.
Who is the animal that makes this lovely shell and feeds many people?
Let's turn the page and find out . . .

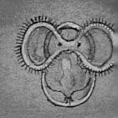

Shelley Conch drifts in the warm ocean.
The waves rock her gently and the ocean
currents carry her.
She has just hatched from a tiny egg and
her clear body is only the size of a speck.
It is hard to believe that she will grow up
to be a Queen Conch, for right now she
doesn't look like a conch at all.
Her body has two round lobes like the
ears of an elephant. Each lobe is rimmed
with fine hairs which beat back and forth -
very fast - and move her up, down and
around in tiny spirals and loops.

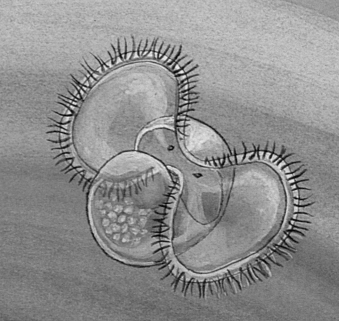

In the sea around Shelley are other tiny creatures.

Some have soft jelly-like bodies and others are glassy-hard.

Some are smooth and others have spines and bristles.

Some will spend their whole lives adrift in the warm seas.

Others, like Shelley, are babies.

They will drift in the sea only while they are very young.

As they grow older they will change their form and live their adult lives on the sea bottom among grasses, rocks, sand or coral reefs.

These drifting animals and plants are called *Plankton*. Plankton means wanderer.

These animals and plants wander far and wide, carried on the currents of the sea.

single celled plants and animals

baby crab

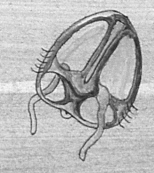

baby jellyfish

baby shrimp

baby fish

baby squid

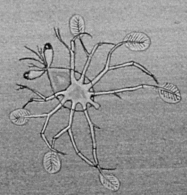

baby crawfish

baby urchin

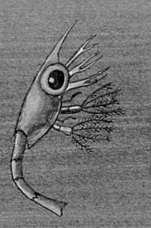

baby hermit crab

To Shelley's small black eyes, creatures the size of a rice grain appear as giant monsters who might eat her up.

These creatures in turn are eaten by larger animals.

The larger animals are eaten by larger ones still.

In this way, the plankton are an important source of food for many animals in the sea from fish to giant whales.

This is why vast numbers of babies hatch from eggs but only a few of these many babies grow up.

Shelley will be very lucky if she can grow up to be a large, pink-lipped conch.

Shelley spends her days drifting and eating.
The beating hairs of her two lobes bring
tasty bits of food to her mouth.
Shelley eats no meat.
She eats only plants.
Each plant she swallows whole, so each
must be small and without hard coatings.
Her favourite plant foods are soft, bite-sized
globes of green.

Shelley drifts about for three weeks.
During this time her two lobes become
four and then six.
Her body is now the size of a sand grain
and she is heavier, too.
She often touches the sea bottom before
bouncing up again.
Shelley settles on the sandy bottom and
now an amazing thing happens.
Over several hours her body changes
form.
Her six lobes shrink and disappear.
Her mouth is now at the end of a long
snout and her eyes are on two stalks!
She is now ready to live on the sea
bottom as older conchs do.

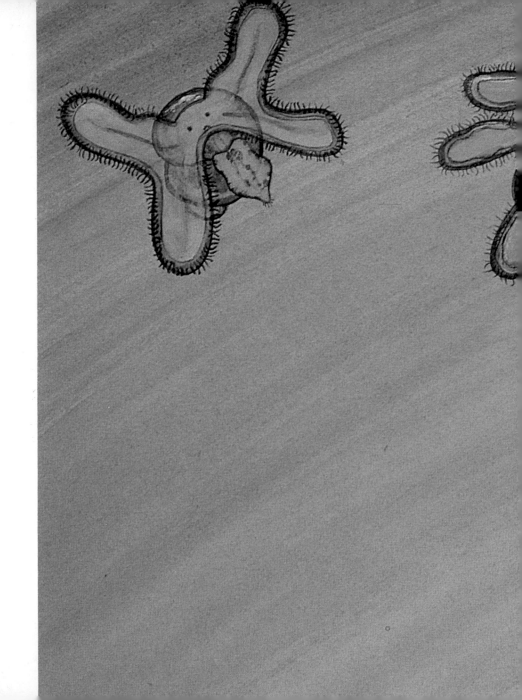

Beneath Shelley's white shell is a strong
little foot and on her foot is a 'claw' like a
large pointed toenail.
With her foot Shelley buries into the sand.
She is so small that many sea creatures
would eat her if they could find her.
Here are some of the many animals which
eat baby conchs...

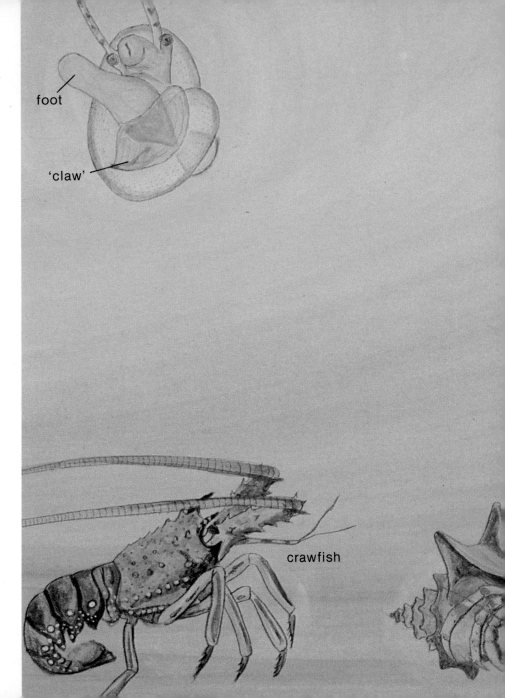

foot

'claw'

crawfish

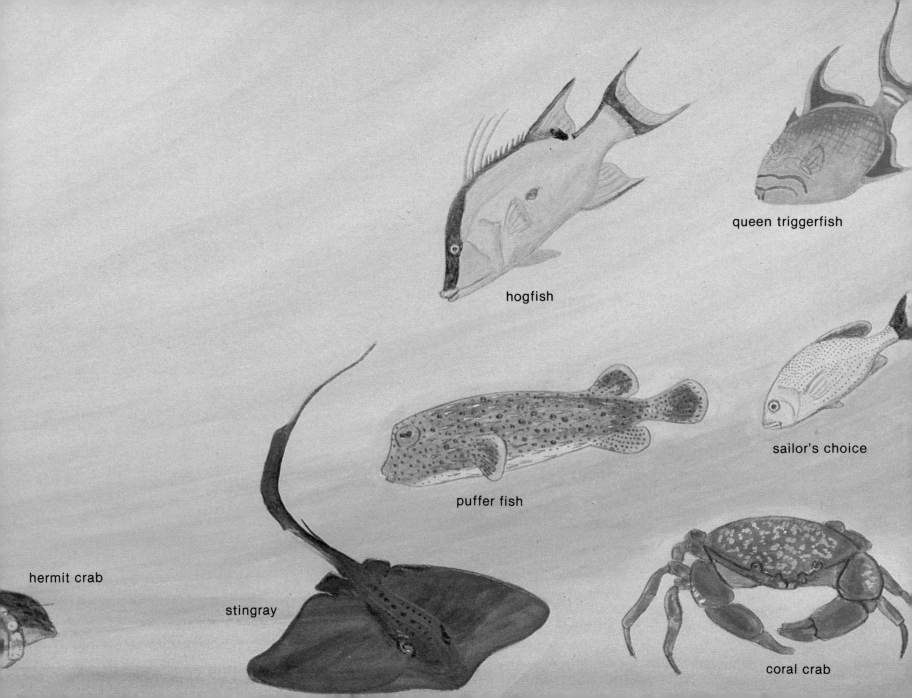

queen triggerfish

hogfish

sailor's choice

puffer fish

hermit crab

stingray

coral crab

So Shelley hides for almost a year in the sand or under weeds.

All the while Shelley is eating and growing.
Her long snout can reach for food and her
special tongue is made for scraping.
With her 'tongue' Shelley scrapes into her
mouth soft tips of seaweeds and plant
films that cover sand grains and grass
blades.
Shelley will eat these plant foods for the
rest of her life.
As Shelley grows she builds her shell larger.
Here's how.
All conchs have an apron of orange skin
called a 'mantle'.
This skin makes a liquid which hardens
into new shell.
Using her mantle, Shelley adds strip after
strip of new shell to the outer edge of her
old shell.
Shelley's body grows in a spiral.
Her shell is a spiral too.
It forms a smooth spiral tube around
Shelley's soft body.
Shelley adds strip after strip of new shell
to the roof of this tube, making the tube
wrap around itself.
With each new strip Shelley builds her
shell spiral larger.

A year passes.
Now Shelley is big enough to move about in the open.
She sees other conchs around her.
Some are her size, others are much larger.
Some of the big conchs have lips that flare out like a spreading skirt.
One day, if Shelley is lucky, she will grow up and build a flared lip on her own shell.

Shelley is growing rapidly.
Her shell is now too thick to be crushed by a
Hog Snapper or a Puffer Fish.
It is a safe home in which she can hide.
Her foot can also protect her.
When a Tulip Snail comes near her with the
plan of eating her for its dinner Shelley kicks
it in the face with her claw and leaps
quickly away.
Both Shelley and the Tulip are kinds of
snails.
They are distant cousins.
But conchs, unlike most snails, have very
good eyesight and can move quickly if they
must.
Conchs, unlike their Tulip Snail cousins, do
not eat meat.

One day a motorboat anchors near the spot
where Shelley sits scraping her breakfast of
soft plant tips.
She sees a strange creature enter the water
in a cloud of bubbles.
He dives down to the bottom and picks up
two large conchs with flared lips.
He starts swimming towards her and
Shelley withdraws her head into the
darkness of her shell.
There is no way she can outrun this diver.

But nothing happens.
When she peers out again he has passed her and is picking up another large conch.
He returns to the boat with his arms full of conchs and climbs out of the water.
Shelley does not know that she is safe from this conch fisherman because she is so small.
The fisherman knows that large conchs have plenty of tasty white meat.
He knows that he must let the little conchs grow bigger.
The fisherman also knows he must leave some adult conchs to breed and lay eggs so there will be more conchs in future years to feed his growing family.

The seasons come and go.
In summer the sea is warm and there is
plenty of food for Shelley and the other
conchs to eat.
Shelley wanders around the grass bed
eating, looking, resting, growing larger, and
building her shell spiral larger, too.

In winter the sea is cooler.
There isn't as much plant food to eat and
Shelley and the other conchs don't move as
much or grow as fast.
Winter storms are common.
During these storms Shelley buries her shell
into the sand and sits without moving,
sometimes for a few days, until it passes.
Sometimes adult conchs with flared lips dig
themselves into the sand and rest quietly for
many weeks.
Sometimes they lie still for so long that they
become covered with sand completely.

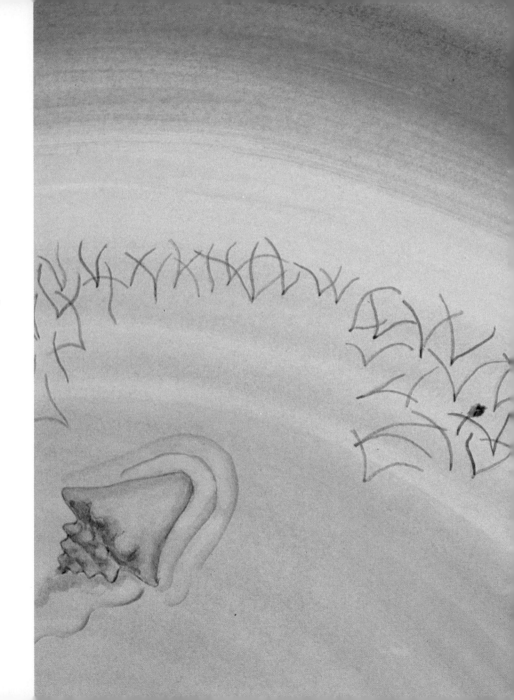

As spring arrives again Shelley is almost full grown.

She is two and a half years old and ready to build a flared lip on her shell.

Instead of adding new shell in a spiral she now adds shell in a new direction – away from her body.

Through spring and early summer she adds more and more shell to her lip until it flares like a skirt.

By mid-summer her lip is complete.

It is thin and fragile with a lovely pink inside.

Now, after nearly three years, Shelley is as large as she will ever be.
Her shell will grow no larger.
Instead, it will grow thicker and thicker.
If Shelley lives to be very old, about six or seven years in all, her shell will have a very thick lip and its outside will look old and worn.

Through autumn and winter Shelley makes her lip stronger and thicker.

Now she is an adult, and one of the biggest conchs in her group.

But she must still keep her amber eyes on watch for enemies who might eat her.

Now her large kicking foot with its curved claw can keep most crabs and Tulip Snails away, but Loggerhead Turtles can crush her strong shell and the Octopus, Stingray and Leopard Ray can still eat large conchs.

This spring when the sea starts to grow
warm Shelley moves away from the grass
bed where she grew up.
Now she moves with other adult conchs.
A male conch with a large shell and thick
flared lip moves close to Shelley.
They sit together with shells touching.
Under the shelter of their two flared lips he
reaches a special arm from his body to hers
and leaves her with many tiny seeds of life.
Later, Shelley will carefully lay a strand of
many, many tiny eggs.
Each one of his seeds will join with one of
her eggs to start a new life.
Shelley will lay six or seven egg masses
before the water turns colder again.

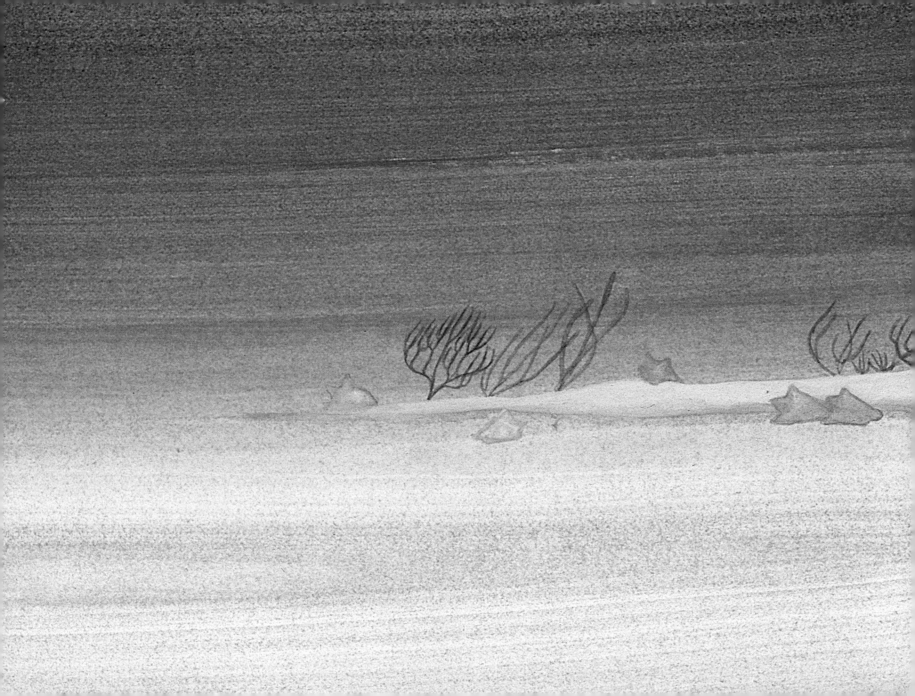

To lay her eggs, Shelley chooses a patch
of clean sand where the sea is fresh.
There she sits quietly.
Down the side of her foot runs a special
groove, and from this groove she lays a
thin strand of clear jelly.
Inside this jelly are thousands of tiny
white eggs.
Each egg is the size of a pinpoint. She
moves her foot back and forth – back and
forth – many times until the strand forms
a mass.
Grains of sand stick to the strand and
when the egg mass is complete it can
hardly be seen.
It looks just like a curved lump of sand.
Shelley leaves her egg mass to hatch by
itself.
She does not need to protect her eggs or
mother her babies.

egg groove

The egg mass sits for three days on the quiet sea bottom.
The egg mass is still, but a tiny new life is swirling inside each egg.
In another day most of the eggs will hatch.
New baby conchs will burst forth into the sea.
They will not look like big conchs yet but with luck a very few of them will live to grow up and have strong shells with lovely pink flared lips.

If we are very careful and leave the conchs in the sea until they have had time to lay eggs, we will always have conchs to eat, conchs to sell, and conchs to make more conchs in the sea.

First published 1984

Published by
Macmillan Publishers
London and Basingstoke
Companies and representatives in Lagos, Zaria,
Manzini, Gaborone, Nairobi, Singapore, Hong Kong,
Delhi, Dublin, Auckland, Melbourne, Tokyo,
New York, Washington, Dallas

ISBN 0 333 38259 5

Printed in Hong Kong